Praise for *Bosk*

Each of these small poems unfolds like a Mallarmé
fan-poem from within the initials of the Latin name
of a bush or tree. While their exact origins are
concealed until the endnotes, each dispatch from the
arboretum is imbued with the spirit of its source-tree.
"Knobby articulations" unfurl themselves like buds
from between the prickles of *crateagus crus-galli*, the
cockspur hawthorn. There are flutters of playful
intimacy in those poems that directly address their
cryptically-named trees, even stronger where
"scattershot rustlings" speak back from the plant
itself, as tree and human find shared voiced in "this
brilliant/ sputtering state of being."

—Ellen Dillon

Patrick Barron's incredible *Bosk* conveys the arbor-
ardors of speech among species. It moves inside the
names we give to nature, pulling word and branch
apart for careful inspection, and drawing out the
secret language that connects tree to tree, and we.
This is a book that reminds us we are all enmeshed in
a "vagrant vacuous whole" across "fields of ever
increasing paratactic parallax."

—Rebecca Kosick

Bosk

Patrick Barron

Unsolicited Press
Portland, Oregon
www.unsolicitedpress.com
info@unsolicitedpress.com
619–354–8005

This collection is a work of poetic imagination. While some poems
draw from personal memory, experience, or lived narrative, others
bend freely toward fiction, dream, or distortion. These verses may
blur fact and feeling, memory and myth—inevitably shaped by the
unreliable nature of perception. Let it be said: at some point, these
poems were inspired by a version of the truth.

Distributed by Asterism Books
https://asterismbooks.com/

For wholesale orders:
Asterism Books
568 1st Avenue South, Ste 120
Seattle, WA 98104
(206) 485-4829
info@asterismbooks.com

Cover art courtesy of the Alan Turner Art Trust
Alan Turner, Untitled, 2000, graphite on paper, 9" x 7"

Editor: Summer Stewart

First lines of poems

Bosk

P

pino I know you
you are close
to my heart
who knows why
amorous whorled
odorous wood
would stir
the emotions so?

k (B)

M

furze guardian
of its own
and our
propriety
stickled armed
pollard
by age or event
or fault
what fruits
do you bear?

s (R)

G

you rake me
over the dead grass
with purple spines
daggers for foragers
with sticky mouths
a porcupine tree
food for a porcupine

v (F)

S

these suicides
branchtips
nervine sanguine
berries and buds
touch me
I'm all fiber
about to fail

s (R)

M

my follicles
are drooping
(so)
please pick
my bushy head
clean
of
red

x r v p (R)

S

an ample ampersand
arrows end
in pinpricks
a tendril
for a sea
of tendrils

x r (S)

Z

(faroff)
hopped out of the hedgerow
willowlinderushesedges
pods become pointed leaves
seedstemstemming
as much
a giant bush
a tree

(upclose)
inchoate home
a trunk become
a throne
rippled edges
frost
besotted green

s (U)

A

A mild luxurious
scabbing
scales unto earth
lichens pepper the crust

b (A)

M

taut globuled yawns
perforate the blue
more berry than bush
jaundiced blisters
brown spotted ceiling
stems
& a den

h (R)

P

ascribbledemise demesne
halfhyphened exhalation
extortion&musing
daresaid day dreamaimed
short of breatheosophy
pritheelapsed syncopatience
tieredification papierpier

s (P)

R

cheeky
rosicrucian glow
flaunts fall
along crookbacked
saddles stems
I'm all addled
altered
angling
for you

x g (E)

M

stippled resistances
until dawn
gelid capsules
bird's last friend
food
from afar
(I'll feed you)

x 'P' (R)

T

ambidextrous hypermobile
shades of green
sunk in selfsame litter
strips of stalk
violet dusky gesticulations
elbows after elbows
knees upon knees

c (T)

O

v for v's sake
seedlings point the way
above an adroit spacing
appendages scattered
to the four+ winds

$v f g$ (B)

C

lapped and luminous perforations
sharp-tongued
soft prongs
protocol of air and light

r (O)

K

shallow temporalities
antonymous parabolas
antigrids over antigrids
how many warps in nexuses
as time bottoms out
and distances venture
far inside of far?

L 'P' (E)

S

green speech
greenness speaking
such an abundance
fusses of needles
in soft clattering
not claptrap canoodling
pattering but
stippled obstinance
in large part the wind
no windows many windows
bowed and bowing fissures
I think I see the sky

G (C)

P

what shape shall
you take next
snaking along
so very many
prepositional shifts
aggregations appearances
derangements departures
in sinuations
that whisper
in minutiae
a slender largesse?

q (V)

S

your interminable waves
over waves of amoral
forms over amoral
images confound one
for the others
overwhelm teetering
ticking twigging
oh to touch
that furzy verge
merging with the light

a x d (S)

A

looping severally slender
trunked signals indicating
future always unkempt flowers
unfurled into fruits
blackish flesh
eaten fresh or
in puddings pies
and muffins or
dried like raisins or
currents and devoured in particular
by songbirds squirrels and bears

a v s (R)

F

there is an affirmation
in this efformation
unfurling reversal
shrinking and generosity
fragments feeling their way
from kernel out of grasping
becoming separatum of separata
a pleasing paraleiptic labyrinth

a (T)

U

how unequal the sides
of your leaves are
and mucilaginous
your bark is
also fragrant gluelike
when chewed through
the outer to the inner
slippery poultice
desiccate and deprive
resurrect and correct
this ailment of speech

r (U)

M

doglegged bearer
of shivering discs
acrid gnawings
of the steppes
offspring who always
take a new form
sheltering if succoring
indifferent fruit

'P' (R)

C

over your imaged form
curved translucence
cornered corneas catch
the blue sky
who
or
what
is to say
prophetically
unwind drops
of drops
from cerise limbs
to spool
off into spongiform
ground

s (C)

C

brachiated bowed
shield you defer
time and again
in whorled tics
rings around rings
knobby articulations
needling needing spines

c-g (R)

Q

wrinkled stigmata
something
skeletal
dark creases
graven yet
not yet
equivocal arrows
at universal dust

a (F)

L

how singularly tapered
deviatingly
undeviatingly
you advance
open conical
in elliptical shedding
light blue green
that turns yellow
hardly undying
roots at right angles
your knees
join
ribs to timbers

l (P)

Q

shelf life extended
by never going straight
loci that veer down
rubberneck up
in the main soaring
in scales
bark
bird song
insect screech
scabrous parchment dawn

v (F)

K

elegiac snakings
doublings back
(abundance and collusions)
temperate contortions
exotic what once
was so familiar
could (at times)
become so estranged
from this maternal thicket

l (E)

C

what remnant
states or acts
enduring correlates
forgotten answers
do your doughty twigs
ruddy ringed nodules
clasp in waxy foliage
antennaed baubles
or are they viruses
cosmoses within
crowded cosmoses
brains lingering
bobbing heads?

O (R)

P

forget me not
purple cowls
cowbells
persistent
underpinnings

t 'C' (S)

U

pixilated awnings
scattershot rustlings
pawings of phalanges
echelons of appendages
over erratic echelons

$$U \text{ `U'} x \ U \ w \text{ `P'} (U)$$

C

amid all the acres
of trestles
and entanglements
your limbs
have the look
of vines

b (B)

P

open and irregular
you droop earthward
slender hairy rough
longing to be prostrate
propagate by layering
unstinted rings
around rings
give rise to
gum and bock

m 'D' (P)

C

rather nonchalant
is what your appearance
seems to bear out
through this uncertain light
a typical archetypal tree

o (J)

C

as the world falls
into itself
there you are
rippled dappled
an ancient thing
whose fruit flickers
over green forks
under the mouth
of the sky
scars where limbs
were lopped off
gyred pitted eyes
each a podium of non sequiturs
solicitous dissembling
nearly transparent

x g (R)

J

simulated, simulating
pointy brows
bowed pin pricks
pallid pellets
bitter biting droplets
of blue, green, grey

v / x m v p (C)

F

as you scab off into
the cool mist
of a year of colors
contained as the container
spills into this instant
chain of instants
you are almost somnolent
your antennae slow to perceive
or so it seems
the slight vibrations
of oranges reds greens yellows
perched on the edge
of incarnation
nearly nonchalant
even if oh so drowsily
cognizant of this brilliant
sputtering state of being

o (F)

C

stalkless leaflets lances
reach out from hairy axes
in slender saw-toothed
pinnate gesturings
that avouch drooping catkins
thin-shelled bitter seeds
bootless but for rabbits
rheumatism and lamps

c (J)

O

wriggling tongues
caught up
in their death
rattle prattle
trip into another life
—on hold

a (E)

M

contortions
that are graceful
rivers that run uphill
downhill
crowns losing their hair
thrones for no
one to care

a 'P' (M)

S

a longing for belonging
pin-pricked air
soon-to-be
stick-riddled
views already suggested
pose over fields
of ever increasing
paratactic parallax

p (O)

F

how many unfolded
folds rest in the
webs of epiphenomena
you find your selves
caught up in
as you wither
whether winter or not?

a (O)

M

the abstraction
waved aside
the rotting
appletiquette
aprodding of branch
tips aplayful
even when at rest
oneupping
doffingofthecap

'G H' (R)

M

absence acquiescence
trailed limber existence
crack marked brachiated
stems get
the better of you
tilted east
milky buds
(pussy willows)
scattershot
future flowers in softness
so early to bed

x l (M)

M

angling-aging
of it all
dome of points
pecked bloodshot pillows
futures dangled
on strings
suicides
not the insides

s R (R)

F

you will shed
your mustard
mottled coat
none too soon
nearly enough
to be alone

s (F)

F

what will you efform
or what into will you
before withering
become immobile
a false impression
and appear to reappear
sublimate or succor
such impulses
must seem natural

n (O)

Q

scabrous echelons
on cellulose scaffolds
a river runs through
sun is shadow
a candelabra muscled dawn
gestures unto gestures

a (F)

A

coppiced bawls
erupt
wide mouthed
fossilized glower
scowl
inexplicable pucker
the multiform
cinnamon parchment

g (S)

S

aqueous lamplit
green flashes
foaming mouths
lakelets
next to platelets
streaming
across shanks
multiform filaments
antlers
cellular collisions
on high

p (T)

G

wide irregular
somewhat wavy
midvein leafstalks
acutely serpentine
spurs and moist cones
maturing and shedding
"living fossil"
"sole survivor"
long cultivated
rancid butter
should not be touched

b (G)

F

phosphorescent
jaundiced dawn
spike scattershot
loss in capture
depth in fields
reversed uprising
rippled waves
touch of
cornea to
cornea

g (O)

U

an isthmus of dripping
nearly not dawn anymore
greenery finery
penciled stems, nodule
to nodule, and leaves
so seriously serrated
they seem utility knives
the cornices of fractals
no nonsense
decoration function

$$\text{'}K\,H\text{'}\,(U\,p\,x\,U\,a)\,(U)$$

S

bulbous riot of flippancy
upright tapering
dome genomes
do their part
the magic is inside
looking up the intestinal core
luminescences
of an arborescence
etched in every pore

r (O)

M

could it be
a hairy enzyme
with a fetor of spring
in the shape of
with a
terror of
blossoms
and fill?

G (C)

T

aromatic poisonous stout
short-pointed
slender flattened flexible
leafstalks shedding plates
sprouting slowly
on bows
in mews
moist ravines
temples and churchyards
your scarlet cups
juicy soft stalkless
can be fatal

c (T)

B

odiferous winter
green ground up twigs
and foliage your long
pointed ellipses
are often notched
at the base
it seems easy to
fall into
your fissures and scaly plates
that augur augers
medicinal fermentation
candy and beer

l (B)

F

for us for those
for all these ovate
slightly sunken
side veins parallel
short stalks
hairless or nearly so
prickly burs
that bear
3-angled kernels
consumed in quantities
by all manner of mammal
your indeterminate bark
preserves
initials and dates
indefinitely

g v c (F)

S

what ails don't you remedy
with those big toothless
mittens pawing the air
promising perfume
and panacea with such pleasant
spicy slight gumminess?

a (L)

H

sidereal xanthous dehiscence
threads upon twisted threads
point to winter astringence
and water

v '*W C*' *(H)*

C

edge tipper tipping into bloom
and beyond
little spoons
spines
pentagram-petaled blossoms
dare you think of picking
without the proper
improper permission

c-g f r (R)

Q

nothing reluctantly
reductively
upright about you
all cantilevered
off kilter
yet countered in equipoise
above
and under
ground

e (F)

J

awash
laved and laving
your clustered tufts
tendrils seek
the ground
as up they go
in no hurry
nearly loathe
to grow

r (C)

A

segmented seeded
cellulose escarpments
fault-blocked bark
osirised sisyphused
snakings of rivulets
each with a parallel
shadow or ineffable crest
the mind and eye
must choose up close
the order of separation
escalates

s (S)

C

ready to wrestle
or recall any
one or thing
you await the end
with stippled
hearts pinned
to your sleeves
ready too
to catch an errant
lost vagrant
vacuous whole

x g (B)

C

let your hair down
drip by drip
chlorophyll
chloroform
acres of air
trestles
and entanglements
your limbs
have the look
of vines

b (B)

P

outstretched episodes
distal distaffs
how much flower power
violet tiny violences
oh so
demented + scintillating

s (R)

C

stereoptic
negative-positives
grey green black
branches
electrocuting blue

m (F)

The Bosk

Pinus koraiensis (Pinaceae)

Malus sylvestris (Rosaceae)

Gleditsia vestita (Fabaceae)

Sorbus scopulina (Rosaceae)

Malus x *robusta* var. *persicifolia* (Rosaceae)

Salix x *rubens* (Salicaceae)

Zelkova schneideriana (Ulmaceae)

Acer buergerianum (Aceraceae)

Malus hupehensis (Rosaceae)

Pinus strobus (Pinaceae)

Rhododendron x *gandavense* (Ericaceae)

Malus x 'Prairifire' (Rosaceae)

Taxus cuspidata (Taxaceae)

Ostrya virginiana f. *glandulosa* (Betulaceae)

Chionanthus retusus (Oleaceae)

Kalmia latifolia 'Polypetala' (Ericaceae)

Sequoiadendron giganteum (Cupressaceae)

Parthenocissus quinquefolia (Vitaceae)

Salix atrocinerea x *discolor* (Salicaceae)

Amelanchier alnifolia var. *semiintegrifolia* (Rosaceae)

Franklinia alatamaha (Theaceae)

Ulmus rubra (Umlaceae)

Malus 'Piotosh'(Rosaceae)

Cornus stolonifera (Cornaceae)

Crataegus crus-galli (Rosaceae)

Quercus alba (Fagaceae)

Larix laricina (Pinaceae)

Quercus velutina (Fagaceae)

Kalmia latifolia (Ericaceae)

Cephalanthus occidentalis (Rubiaceae)

Paulownia tomentosa 'Coreana' (Scrophulariaceae)

Ulmus 'Urban' x *Ulmus wilsoniana* 'Patriot'
         (Ulmaceae)

Catalpa bungei (Bignoniaceae)

Picea mariana 'Doumetii' (Pinaceae)

Carya ovata (Juglandaceae)

Crataegus x *grignonensis* (Rosaceae)

Juniperus virginiana / x *media* var. *pfitzeriana*
         (Cupressaceae)

Fagus orientalis (Fagaceae)

Carya cordiformis (Juglandaceae)

Oxydendrum arboreum (Ericaceae)

Morus alba 'Pendula' (Moraceae)

Syringa pekinensis (Oleaceae)

Fraxinus americana (Oleaceae)

Malus 'Golden Hornet' (Rosaceae)

Magnolia x *loebneri* (Magnoliaceae)

Malus sargentii Rehder (Rosaceae)

Fagus sylvatica (Fagaceae)

Fraxinus nigra (Oleaceae)

Quercus alba (Fagaceae)

Acer griseum (Sapindaceae)

Stewartia pseudocamellia (Theaceae)

Ginkgo biloba (Ginkgoaceae)

Forsythia giraldiana (Oleaceae)

Ulmus 'Kansas Hybrid' (*U. pumila* x *U. americana*)
       (Ulmaceae)

Syringa reticulata (Oleaceae)

Metasequoia glyptostroboides (Cupressaceae)

Taxus canadensis (Taxaceae)

Betula lenta (Betulaceae)

Fagus grandifolia var. *caroliniana* (Fagaceae)

Sassafras albidum (Lauraceae)

Hamamelis virginiana 'Winter
Champagne'(Hamamelidaceae)

Crataegus crus-galli f. *rubens* (Rosaceae)

Quercus ellipsoidalis (Fagaceae)

Juniperus rigida (Cupressaceae)

Acer saccharum (Sapindaceae)

Catalpa x *galleana* (Bignoniaceae)

Catalpa bungei (Bignoniaceae)

Prunus serotina (Rosaceae)
Castanea mollissima (Fagaceae)

Note

The short poems in *Bosk* can be read as cued accounts of woody plants carefully observed from afar and up close. The initials of the plants' Latin names that frame the poems are listed at the end of the book. Most of the encounters described here took place in the Arnold Arboretum in Boston, many in the company of Piero or Giacomo while they were napping.

About Patrick Barron

Writer and translator Patrick Barron grew up in the Pacific Northwest, moving from Great Falls, Montana to Anchorage, Alaska, and then Eugene, Oregon. He spent significant years in Belfast, Northern Ireland, Ferrara, Italy, and San Francisco, and holds degrees in both English and Cultural Geography. He now lives in Boston where he teaches at the University of Massachusetts. His books include *Spooring* (poetry); *Selected Essays and Dialogues: Adventures into the Errant Familiar*, by Gianni Celati; *Terrain Vague: Interstices at the Edge of the Pale*; *Haiku for a Season, Haiku per una stagione*, by Andrea Zanzotto; *The Selected Poetry and Prose of Andrea Zanzotto*; and *Italian Environmental Literature: An Anthology*. His work has received a number of recognitions, including the Rome Prize; the National Endowment for the Arts Translation Fellowship; the National Endowment for the Humanities Fellowship; the Raiziss/de Palchi Translation Award; and a Fulbright Scholarship.

About the Press

Unsolicited Press is based out of Portland, Oregon and focuses on the works of the unsung and underrepresented. As a womxn–owned, all–volunteer small publisher that doesn't worry about profits as much as championing exceptional literature, we have the privilege of partnering with authors skirting the fringes of the lit world. We've worked with emerging and award–winning authors such as Sommer Schafer, Amy Shimshon–Santo, Brook Bhagat, Mari Matthias, and Amy Baskin. Learn more at unsolicitedpress.com. Find us on Twitter and Instagram at @UnsolicitedP.